Create and Share · Thinking Digitally

Being a Team Player Online

By Amber Lovett

Published in the United States of America by:
CHERRY LAKE PRESS
2395 South Huron Parkway, Suite 200, Ann Arbor, Michigan
www.cherrylakepublishing.com

Series Adviser: Kristin Fontichiaro
Reading Adviser: Marla Conn, MS, Ed., Literacy specialist, Read-Ability, Inc.
Book Designer: Felicia Macheske
Character Illustrator: Rachael McLean

Photo Credits: © Monkey Business Images/Shutterstock.com, 5; © Pavel L Photo and Video/Shutterstock.com, 13; © Kanghophoto/Shutterstock.com, 15; © Yuriy Golub/Shutterstock.com, 17; © wavebreakmedia/Shutterstock.com, 19; © Sam Wordley/Shutterstock.com, 20

Graphics Throughout: © the simple surface/Shutterstock.com; © Diana Rich/Shutterstock.com; © lemony/Shutterstock.com; © CojoMoxon/Shutterstock.com; © IreneArt/Shutterstock.com; © Artefficient/Shutterstock.com; © Marie Nimrichterova/Shutterstock.com; © Svetolk/Shutterstock.com; © EV-DA/Shutterstock.com; © briddy/Shutterstock.com; © Mix3r/Shutterstock.com

Copyright © 2020 by Cherry Lake Publishing
All rights reserved. No part of this book may be reproduced or utilized in any form or by any means without written permission from the publisher.

Library of Congress Cataloging-in-Publication Data

Names: Lovett, Amber, author. | McLean, Rachael, illustrator.
Title: Being a team player online / by Amber Lovett ; illustrated by Rachael McLean.
Description: Ann Arbor, Michigan : Cherry Lake Publishing, 2020. | Series: Create and share : thinking digitally | Includes index. | Audience: Grades 2-3.
Identifiers: LCCN 2019033482 (print) | LCCN 2019033483 (ebook) | ISBN 9781534159143 (hardcover) | ISBN 9781534161443 (paperback) | ISBN 9781534160293 (pdf) | ISBN 9781534162594 (ebook)
Subjects: LCSH: Internet games—Juvenile literature. | Cooperation—Juvenile literature.
Classification: LCC GV1469.15 .L68 2020 (print) | LCC GV1469.15 (ebook) | DDC 794.8/1—dc23
LC record available at https://lccn.loc.gov/2019033482
LC ebook record available at https://lccn.loc.gov/2019033483

Cherry Lake Publishing would like to acknowledge the work of the Partnership for 21st Century Learning, a Network of Battelle for Kids. Please visit www.battelleforkids.org/networks/p21 for more information.

Printed in the United States of America
Corporate Graphics

Table of Contents

CHAPTER ONE
It's All About Teamwork 4

CHAPTER TWO
Playing Games Online 8

CHAPTER THREE
Start a Gaming League 14

CHAPTER FOUR
What's Next? 18

GLOSSARY 22
FOR MORE INFORMATION 23
INDEX 24
ABOUT THE AUTHOR 24

CHAPTER ONE

It's All About Teamwork

Imagine playing a game of tag by yourself or building a tree house without help. The game of tag wouldn't make sense. And building that tree house would be close to impossible! Working together can make things easier and more fun. Each person has a different role or job to do when working on a team. People team up online to do things too. Let's find out how!

There are many ways people work together online. You and your friends can play games or work together on a school project online. Remember to talk to a trusted adult before you go online. Never give out personal information, even to your friends. If you aren't sure what is okay to share, ask an adult first. You can't have fun online if you aren't safe!

Tic-tac-toe isn't much fun without a friend to play with.

Your parents or teachers can help you stay safe online.

ACTIVITY

What Is Safe to Share Online?

Copy this list to a sheet of paper. Then put a check mark in the "Private: Do Not Share" column or the "Okay to Share" column.

INFORMATION	PRIVATE: DO NOT SHARE	OKAY TO SHARE
Your last name	?	?
Your address and phone number	?	?
Your school's name or address	?	?
Pictures of yourself	?	?
Your nickname	?	?
What you think or know about a particular topic	?	?
Your **email address**	?	?
Your pet's name	?	?

Did you mark the first four items on the list as private? These things should never be shared online. The last four items on the list are usually okay to share.

Teaming up online is a lot of work and comes with some responsibility. It is hard to tell what others are feeling when you don't see them. Your team might not know when you're joking. Sometimes people's feelings are hurt by accident. This is why communication is important. Using kind words—and sometimes even **emojis**—can help.

Good team members know how to work together. Think about the other person's feelings and opinions. Remember that in a team, everyone is important. You should treat others the way you would want to be treated.

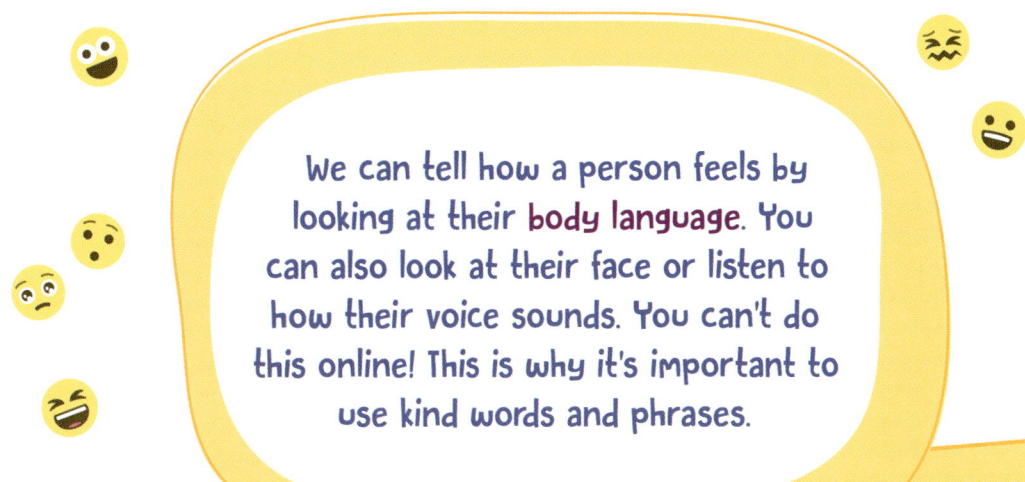

We can tell how a person feels by looking at their **body language**. You can also look at their face or listen to how their voice sounds. You can't do this online! This is why it's important to use kind words and phrases.

CHAPTER TWO

Playing Games Online

Do you like playing games? There are a lot of games you can play online! Some games are free, and some cost money. Some games are for kids, but many are not. It's important to talk to a trusted adult before choosing an online game.

There are many different games. Some games you can play alone. Some you can play with friends or strangers. Some games let you build and explore new worlds. These are called **sandbox games**. There are also action, adventure, puzzle, and sports games. And many more!

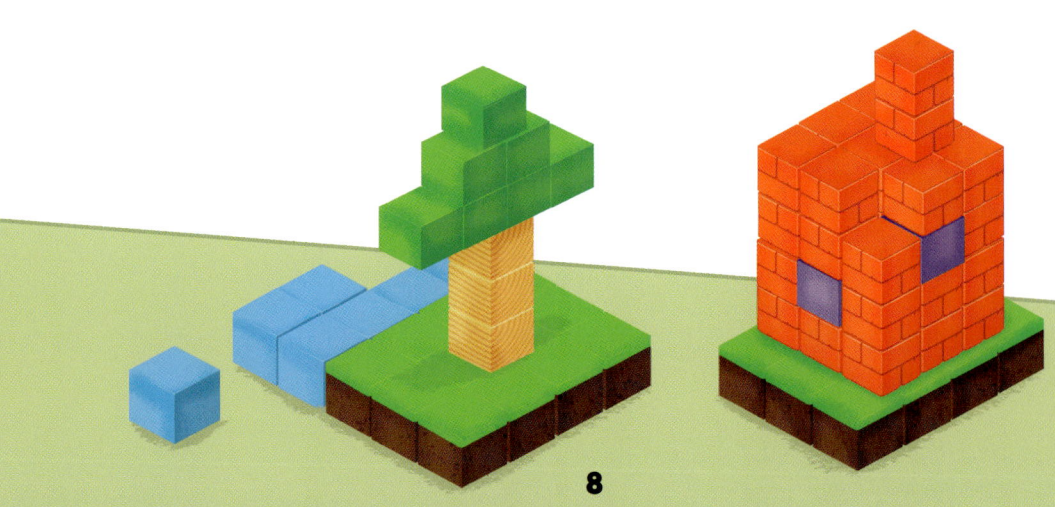

Once you and your friends decide on a game to play, you may need to create an **account**. To do this, sometimes you need to enter an email address. Always ask an adult before signing up for anything online.

Once you're all set up, you and your friends can team up!

Minecraft's Creative mode lets you build your own worlds.

Some games may ask you to create a **gamertag**. This is the name you use to play online. Make sure the gamertag you choose does not contain personal information or bad words. Need help thinking of a name? Think about hobbies or interests you have. You can make a tag based on a favorite show, song, or movie. You can also use the names of your pets or a nickname. You might use numbers in your tag. It is better to choose random numbers, not numbers that are special to you. Just remember that everyone can see your tag! Don't choose a tag that might hurt someone's feelings or give away your personal information.

Some games are rated, just like movies.
Look for games rated E (Everyone).

ACTIVITY

What Game Should I Play?

Not sure what kind of online game to play? Use the list below to help you choose. Sign up for the game and choose a gamertag. Share your gamertag with your friends and ask for theirs. Then you can play together!

IF YOU LIKE...

OVERCOMING OBSTACLES	BUILDING NEW WORLDS	STRETCHING MY BRAIN
Planning	Being creative	Planning
Thinking quickly	Discovering new things	Piecing things together
Physical challenges	**Open-ended** games	Paying attention to detail

THEN YOU SHOULD PLAY...

An action game	A sandbox game	A puzzle game

One word to remember when working online is SMART. SMART stands for safety, manners, adult **supervision**, responsibility, and teamwork. Think about each of these things when you go online. Being SMART online will help you stay safe.

Do you need help choosing a game? Ask an adult to help you search and read reviews from various websites.

CHAPTER THREE

Start a Gaming League

Playing online games with friends is fun. What's even more fun is when you are on the same team online *and* in the same room. You can do this by starting an online gaming league with your friends.

There are professional video game players and leagues that organize esports **competitions**. Esports, or electronic sports, is similar to sports you play in the real world, like soccer. Like soccer, an esports league plays and trains together and competes in front of large crowds. The best gamers and teams win prizes and move on to bigger competitions!

You can start a Minecraft league with your friends!

You can start your own esports league with your friends. You can play together and help each other become better gamers. Watching your friends play is a great way to learn new strategies and hidden codes, called **cheat codes**. Cheat codes can make playing games easier, but they aren't really cheating. These codes are designed by **game developers** to help test the games they made.

> The people who make games are called game developers. Game developers write the computer codes that make games work. Game testers test games to make sure they work right. If you like computers and video games, you might want to be a game developer or tester one day, too!

ACTIVITY

Plan Your League

Ask your parents if you can have your friends over to form a gaming league. With your friends, you can come up with a plan for your league. Use this list to help you plan with your parents and friends.

- When will our league meet? How often?
- Where will we meet?
- What games will we play?
- What will our league be called?
- Who will we invite to our league?
- What are the rules for our league?

Esports leagues take place all over the world.

CHAPTER FOUR

What's Next?

You've started playing with friends online and discovered how to work together as a team. So what's next? It's always a good idea to pause and reflect on your experience and what you have learned. How is working together online different? Is playing games online more fun than in person? What were the challenges working with others online? Thinking about these questions can help you become a better team player both online and offline!

Now that you have played one game, you might be ready to try another one. If you think you aren't very good yet, think about how to improve. Remember, practice counts! And you might want to add more friends to your gaming league. Whatever you do, remember to be safe and SMART online!

What have you learned about teamwork?

Safety is number one! Always ask an adult if you have questions about how to be safe online.

ACTIVITY

SMART

Remember to be SMART when teaming up online. Use this checklist to make sure you don't miss any tips:

SAFETY
- I did not share private information.
- I told an adult if I was asked to share private information.

MANNERS
- I used polite and kind words in my posts.
- I treated others like I would want to be treated.

ADULT SUPERVISION
- I asked an adult for permission before going online.
- I asked an adult to help me sign up for the games I wanted to play.

RESPONSIBILITY
- I realize that I am responsible for everything I have posted.
- I reported any **inappropriate** online content to an adult right away.

TEAMWORK
- I shared the lead and took turns.
- I offered help to my teammates.
- I remembered to include others.

GLOSSARY

account (uh-KOUNT) a requirement some websites have where they ask for your personal information before allowing you into the site; it usually requires a username and password

body language (BAH-dee LANG-gwij) how we use our bodies to communicate without words

cheat codes (CHEET KOHDZ) directions in a computer language that unlock special features in video games

competitions (kahm-puh-TISH-uhnz) events where people try to do better than each other to win prizes

email address (EE-mayl uh-DRES) an address that people can send mail to online

emojis (ih-MOH-jeez) small images or symbols used in text messages or online to express emotions

game developers (GAME dih-VEL-uhp-urz) the people who make video games

gamertag (GAME-ur-tahg) the name that gamers use online

inappropriate (in-uh-PROH-pree-it) not right or proper for the situation, time, or place

obstacles (AHB-stuh-kuhlz) things that make it difficult to do something

open-ended (oh-puhn-END-id) having no limits or no fixed answer

sandbox games (SAND-bahks GAYMZ) video games that let you change and explore the game's world

supervision (soo-pur-FIZH-uhn) the act of watching over someone or something

For More INFORMATION

BOOKS

Cornwall, Phyllis. *Play It Safe Online*. Ann Arbor, Michigan: Cherry Lake Publishing, 2012.

Jennings, Brien J. *Stay Safe Online*. North Mankato, Minnesota: Capstone, 2018.

WEBSITES

Azoomee—E-Safety with Azoomee
http://azoomee.com/index.php/searchitup
Watch videos and take quizzes about the internet and online safety. Or ask a parent if you can use the Azoomee app to help you team up online.

Safe Search Kids
https://www.safesearchkids.com
Search and read about how to be safe online.

INDEX

accounts, **online**, 9
address, **email**, 9

body language, 7

cheat codes, 16
competitions, 14

email address, 9
emojis, 7
esports, 14, 16

feelings, 7

game developers, 16
gamertag, 10
games, **online**
  See online games

information, **personal**, 4, 10

kindness, 7

leagues, **gaming**, 14–17

manners, 12, 21
Minecraft, 9, 15

online
  safety, 5, 12, 20, 21
  what's safe to share, 6
  working together, 4–7
online games, 4, 8–13
  choosing, 11, 13
  developers, 16
  practicing, 18
  ratings, 10
  SMART, 12, 18
  starting a league, 14–17
  testers, 16
  working together, 18–21

practice, 18

responsibility, 7, 12, 21

safety, 5, 12, 20, 21
sandbox games, 8
sharing, **online**, 6
SMART, 12, 18, 21
supervision, **adult**, 12, 21

tags, 10
teamwork, 4–7, 12, 21
tester, **online games**, 16

About the AUTHOR

Amber Lovett is a certified school librarian and teacher. She lives with her husband, Karan, in Portland, Oregon.